Javier Builds a Bridge

A Civil Engineering Story

Written by the Engineering is Elementary Team
Illustrated by Jeannette Martin

| Chapter One | # The Crossing |

"Javi, wait for me!" my little stepsister whined—but I kept running. Reaching the riverbank, I leaped onto the rope and plank footbridge. It wobbled and rocked side to side under my feet. I jumped off the bridge and grabbed the sweet gum tree branch hanging low over my head. I dangled and then let myself drop onto the pebbly bank, ready to run. I couldn't wait to get to my fort. I wanted to finish painting it before the big family party we were having the next day. Everyone was coming to our house in Texas to celebrate the anniversary of Abuelita and Abuelito, my grandparents.

"Javi!" Luisa called. I wanted to leave her there, but something made me stop. I turned around. At the opposite bank, she put a little white sneaker on a plank of the bridge and pulled it back. The bridge was still swaying from my leap. Her face was wet with tears.

I groaned. "Don't you want to go color? You can use my markers."

"Javi!" she sniffled.

"All right, wait a second." I walked back to take her hand. The stream flowed brown beneath us. Luisa peered between the boards. Her body stiffened as she watched the water.

"Come on, you're a big girl," I said—but I was really thinking about how little she was. Being a new big brother wasn't always as much fun as I had thought it would be. Before Mamá married Joe, I used to be able to play by myself on the island. Now Joe's daughter Luisa followed me everywhere.

Luisa was inching slowly across the bridge. I was in a hurry. "Look, Luisa, why don't you let me carry you the rest of the way?" I asked. I bent down to pick her up but she pulled away. The bridge tottered and lurched. *Plunk! Splash!* We were in the water!

Chapter Two | A Hero's Reward?

The water wasn't that deep for me, but Luisa was struggling. She coughed and sobbed. Moving as fast as I could, I scooped her out of the stream. I carried her the whole way home as she cried and cried. Mamá would not be happy about this.

Everyone came running when we got to the lawn—Mamá from her art studio; Abuelita and Abuelito from the house; and my stepfather, Joe, from the shed. After I told them what happened, they gave us both hugs and had us change our clothes. By dinnertime, though, I was arguing myself to the edge of big trouble.

"Mamá, it's not fair! Why should I have to stop going to my fort just because Luisa fell in the water?"

"Javier," Mamá said in her sternest voice, "the bridge is just not safe—for her or for you. What if one of you had hit your head on a rock? That bridge is coming down."

"Luisa's safe now," I cried. "It's not fair to punish me!"

"Javier! No more arguments."

I shot a look at Joe, pleading with my eyes. He was my last hope. "Javi, your mamá is right," he said. "We're not punishing you. We're just keeping everyone safe."

"But—" I began.

Mamá banged my plate on the table—my last warning. I couldn't believe I wouldn't be able to go out to the island. All because I had a little sister now. I grabbed my fork and picked at my rice.

Chapter Three | An Idea

Sulking in my room, I heard the four grown-ups talking in low voices. Were they talking about me? I crept down the hallway to listen.

Luisa saw me when I passed her room. "Play with me?" she asked.

I definitely was not in the mood to play with her. She pointed to the blocks in front of her. "Look! A road and buildings and a lake!" Her road had stopped at the lake. What she needed, of course, was a bridge to get over it. One of the rectangle blocks would do. I sighed. I was tired of bridges.

Hey…wait a second! The idea came to me like the sun breaking out after a storm. I picked up some of the blocks. "I'll be right back, Luisa, okay?" I called as I dashed to the kitchen to share my idea.

"We don't have to tear down the bridge," I announced. "I could make a safer one instead!"

Mamá put down a hand on her hip and opened her mouth to speak, but Joe's voice broke in.

"What a good idea!" he said. "How come I didn't think of that? With some good technology, I'm sure we can solve this problem."

I was hoping Joe would like my idea. Joe is a civil engineer. Engineers design things or ways of getting stuff done, using what they know about science, math, and creative thinking. Joe helps design big structures, such as dams, roads, and buildings. He taught me that all of those structures, and any other things that people design to solve problems, are technology.

"That sounds like an awfully difficult project, Javi," Abuelita said.

Abuelito put one of his big, tanned hands on my shoulder. "But this is an awfully smart grandson we have. Tell us what you have in mind."

"Well," I said, "the bridge we have now is made of planks of wood and rope. It's really wobbly. That's why we lost our balance on it yesterday. We need a bridge that's sturdy."

"Yeah," Joe added, scratching his head. "You need something nice and stable, something that can't be knocked off balance when you walk on it or shift your weight."

"This'll be easy!" I said. "Look. I'll show you."

Chapter Four | Complications

I placed two of the blocks I had grabbed from Luisa's room a few inches apart on the table. Then I laid another block across the gap between them. "See? The new bridge could be a plank of wood, or a tree trunk!" I imagined myself walking across the bridge. "It would be stable. It wouldn't bounce around."

Joe was still scratching his head. "That's a great start. Beam bridges like that are nice and simple," he said. "A stiff board will help keep the bridge from wobbling when your weight pushes down on just one side."

"Joe," said Mamá, "that's a wide crossing. Wouldn't you need a few boards to cross the stream? Then you'd have to build supports right into the riverbed. That's a lot of work and maintenance."

"Your Mamá might be right," Joe said. "The length that a bridge can go without anything holding it up in the middle is called the span. The stream is so wide that a beam bridge might need supports—we call those piers—to go all the way across the water."

My shoulders sagged.

Joe said, "Don't worry, Javier. This is what I go through all the time when I start a new project at work. We're asking questions about how to solve the problem. It's the first step of the engineering design process." He winked. "This is how we engineers design things, you know?"

"Well, I'm sure that between you and Joe, you'll think of something, Javi," Abuelito said.

"That's right. I'm sure of it!" agreed Abuelita. Mamá still looked skeptical, but she nodded, too.

"How about if you think of some more questions on your own?" Joe said. "Figure out what you already know about bridges you've seen, how you think they might work, and how you can use that to solve our engineering problem. Then move onto the next step—imagining lots of different ideas. When you think you have a good list, figure out which idea you think will work best. Come up with a simple plan, and then Mamá and I will help you build the bridge. Just don't make a plan that will be too expensive!"

I picked up the smooth block and rubbed it in my hand. Thanks to that block, I'd be able to go to my fort after all.

Food for Thought

"There you are!" Mamá came through the doorway of Luisa's room early the next morning. I was using blocks to help me think of bridge ideas.

"Want to see my ideas?" I handed her my stack of drawings, five in all.

Mamá tipped her head and peered at the papers. "Oh, nice. I like this green one."

"Yeah, I like that one, too. But all of them are beam bridges. I need a new idea."

Mamá nodded. "I know what that's like. When I get stuck with my artwork," she said, "sometimes I just take a break—put the problem out of my mind and let my imagination rest. Want to leave all this for a while and help us make tamales?"

Tamales! I had forgotten. This afternoon we were having a big family party for Abuelito and Abuelita's 50th wedding anniversary. My nose tingled with the scent of onions, tomatoes, and hot peppers as I followed Mamá to the kitchen.

"How's our young engineer?" Abuelito asked. He sat at the table while Abuelita spooned the special batter of corn *masa* into sheets of corn husks, and Luisa helped spread it flat. I gave everyone an update on my bridge, but soon we were talking about the party. My two favorite cousins were coming: Manny, from San Francisco, and Jennifer, from Tennessee.

"That'll be great!" I said, putting a dollop of spicy sauce on the *masa*. "For once, there will be someone around who's fun to play with!"

Suddenly, the adults were quiet. Abuelito cleared his

throat. "Javier, listen up. Do you know what I like most about bridges?"

"No, what?"

"I like what they do. Imagine a person on one side of a valley and someone on the other side. What happens when they build a bridge across the gap?"

I shrugged. "They can cross over to each other."

"That's right, Javi," Abuelito said. "Bridges bring people together. You need to practice being a good bridge builder."

"I'll build the new bridge really well," I said.

"It's not the new bridge I'm talking about. It's your family. You can bring them together."

"People can't build bridges without kind words and patience," Abuelita added. "Those are your tools now."

What were they talking about? I wondered.

Chapter Six | Brainstorming Bridges

       The party started a few hours later. I waited restlessly for Manny and Jennifer to arrive. "C'mon! I have something to tell you!" I pulled them away from the loud music, the laughter, and the long tables of food. Luisa was on our heels.

       In my bedroom I told my cousins the whole story of falling into the stream and what had happened next. "And now," I said, "I get to design a new bridge! But I need your help figuring out how to do it."

       "I help, too!" Luisa exclaimed.

       "No, Luisa, you're too little!" my cousin Manny shouted. Manny's sharpness surprised me. Luisa looked surprised, too. Her chin wrinkled like she might cry. I thought about what Abuelito had said before. *Luisa just wants to be big, like the rest of us*, I realized. Maybe I'm supposed to build a bridge to bring her closer to me.

"Well, maybe she can help a little," I told Manny. "We can pretend." They nodded.

"So we need some ideas," I said. "Do you know any famous bridges we could copy?"

"Ooh, I know a good one," Jennifer said.

"I know one, too," said Manny. "I bet mine's better."

"Mine's the Natchez Trace Bridge," Jennifer said. "My family drove over it when we visited Mississippi on vacation." She sketched a line with two humps underneath it like a curvy M. "We read the plaque at the rest area. Mom said these arch things are supposed to be really strong. When the weight of the car pushes down on the road," she explained, "the supports on the side—they're called

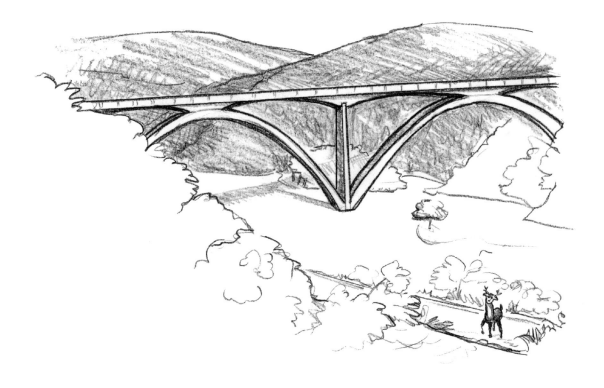

abutments—push in. Anyway, the bridge won a design award for how it looks. I think it's the best bridge in the whole world!"

Manny replied, "Not the best-best, though. Mine's the best-best. It's the Golden Gate Bridge, where I live. Everyone who visits San Francisco goes to see it." He drew two big towers with cables hanging between them like streamers. "It's a hanging bridge—I mean, a suspension bridge. These cables are like suspenders keeping somebody's pants up."

"What about you, Javier? What bridges do you know?" Jennifer asked.

I shrugged. "I drew a picture of the longest bridge I've ever seen. We drove over it when we went to Louisiana. It's just like all the other bridges I've been drawing."

"I made a bridge, too!" Luisa said. She explained her scribbles and splotches. "Trees, rope swing, a fairy house! That's Javi!"

"Oh, nice, Luisa," Jennifer said. She looked at me and Manny. "What now? I don't think it'll work to mix all these ideas together."

"Let's build my bridge," Manny said.

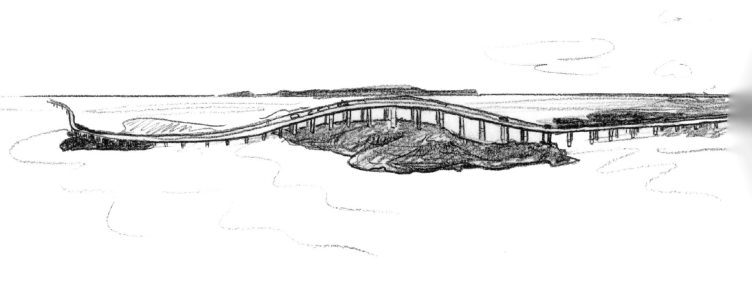

"Manny." Jennifer put a hand on her hip. "How are we supposed to get cables and make the towers? The bridge has to work in real life, you know."

"But your arch bridge is going to be hard to build, too," Manny said. "How would we even make the arch?"

"So, we'll try Javier's idea, then," Jennifer suggested.

"No—I only drew this because I can't think of anything else," I said. "Mamá already said it might not work, because we'd need to build extra supports in the river."

My cousins fell quiet. Luisa kept talking.

"See my drawing, Javi? Trees, water, swing, bird, and . . ." This time I paid attention.

Luisa showed me a line and a scribble for the tire swing hanging from a tree branch, right next to the river. There was a stick figure, hanging from a different tree branch. It reminded me of how I would grab the branches at the edge of the rope and plank bridge. I took another look at Manny's drawing of the hanging bridge.

"Hey," I said, "look at that! Luisa gave me an idea! We can use rope for a cable to make a bridge like Manny's. What'd you call it?"

"A suspension bridge," Manny said, grinning.

Jennifer was squinting at the drawings. "I still don't get how we are going to build those towers."

"We don't need to," I said. "We can use the trees on the river bank, and hang rope across—like a clothesline." I sketched the details. "We can hang the bridge from the rope!" It took a second for Jennifer to picture what I meant, but then she nodded.

"Now all we have to do is figure out how to make it work," she said.

Our hands got busy. We chattered with new ideas.

"Let's test it out with chairs as the trees!"

"Where should we put the strings?"

"How're we going to attach them?"

We figured out the basic idea. Then we collected string and cardboard. When we were done, we tested our model with one of my toy cars.

As soon as we put the car down, the whole bridge buckled and tipped.

"Oh, no!" I said, remembering when Luisa and I fell into the river. "Joe'll never let us build that. He said a bridge shouldn't be thrown off balance when weight's put on it."

Jennifer crouched near the bridge where the car had fallen off. "Maybe it's okay. I think we only need to move the string around. It should pull up here where the car was pushing down too hard."

We went back to work and improved the bridge. We decided where to add more strings and paid attention to pulling up on the bridge where the weight of the cars would push down. We went back and forth between planning our new ideas and making and trying the model bridge. We even let Luisa put the test cars on the bridge.

"One, two, three, four, five!" she counted them out, and we all cheered. At last, our bridge seemed strong enough.

Jennifer said, "Now we have to make a railing so Luisa

stays safe." We brainstormed ideas and finally decided to weave strings between the suspenders. This bridge was getting better and better. At last it was time for Joe to check out the idea and tell us if he approved.

Chapter Seven | Joe Weighs In

Somehow we managed to pull Abuelito and Abuelita away from the crowd to show them the bridge we had built. Mamá and Joe joined us. They huddled around the bridge as we demonstrated its strength.

"Interesting!" Joe nodded and smiled. "How did you come up with this idea?"

"Well," I began, "Luisa's drawing reminded me that there are trees near the riverbanks—trees we can use as the towers of a suspension bridge. The suspension bridge was Manny's idea. All we need is rope—"

"Strong rope," Jennifer said.

"Or maybe metal chains," Manny added.

"Then we make a real bridge that will be stable enough

for Luisa and me to cross. I think we can even use the rope and plank bridge we already have to make the roadbed. We'll just hang it so it will be nice and straight and steady."

"And make railings or something for the sides, so no one can fall off!" Jennifer said.

Abuelita clapped her hands. Abuelito patted me on the back. Mamá said quietly, "Well, how about that?"

Manny and Jennifer chattered, explaining how we

tested our ideas. But Joe was quietly scratching his head, thinking, thinking. What would he say? I held my breath.

"Joe?" I asked, not wanting to wait any longer.

"This is a really neat idea," he began slowly, as I waited with a pounding heart. "I think . . ." He looked serious and paused. Then, with a big grin, he said, "I can't wait to start building!"

Joe promised to help me figure out an exact plan for the real bridge, including how much chain we would need. Then we would build a first version, which Joe called a prototype, together.

"And if it doesn't work just right," Joe cautioned, "we'll have to improve it until it's okay. No using the new bridge until it's safe. Deal?"

"Deal!" I said.

"What a great idea you and your cousins had, Javi," Mamá said.

"No, Mamá, it wasn't just us," I corrected her. "It was us and my sister. The trees were her idea, right, Luisa?" Luisa grinned back at me.

Chapter Eight | A Second Crossing

Four weeks later, I packed three tuna sandwiches and one peanut butter and jelly without the crust into a bag. I let Luisa carry the bag and I carried a backpack of juice boxes and bottles of water.

"Shhhh," I said, tiptoeing over to the cupboard where the birthday candles were.

"Shhhhh," she answered.

I picked up the cake that Mamá had made for dessert. We left a note on the kitchen table and set out for our adventure.

Several minutes later, we used a walkie-talkie to call Mamá. I held the button for Luisa and told her what to say:

"Go to the kitchen and follow directions!"

We waited for Mamá and Joe at the foot of the new suspension bridge. It stretched across the river, hanging from trees and metal chains. When they saw us, they waved. Joe called out, "What's this about?"

"Happy birthday!" called Luisa. "Surprise!"

"Birthday?" Mamá and Joe looked at each other. "It's nobody's birthday," Mamá said.

"Nope, but it's been six months that we've been a family together. That's like a birthday!" I grinned. "Let's celebrate at our fort!"

We marched across the bridge, one after the other. At the fort, we gobbled up the lunch, and Joe lit the candles on the cake. We all closed our eyes to wish before blowing them out. I had my fort back and a happy family—all my wishes had come true. I laughed and watched the rest of my family instead.

Design A Bridge

Have you ever made bridges out of blocks? Have you ever had to make a bridge over a real stream like Javier did? Your goal is to design the strongest bridge that you can using paper and cardboard.

Materials
- ☐ Index cards or construction paper
- ☐ Heavy blocks and heavy books
- ☐ Long strips of cardboard, about eight inches wide
- ☐ String or yarn
- ☐ Clothes pins with springs or paper clips
- ☐ Duct tape or packing tape

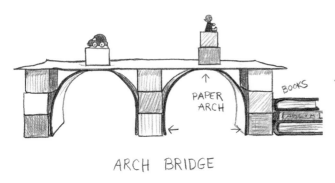

ARCH BRIDGE

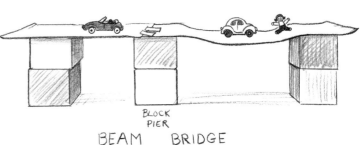

BEAM BRIDGE

Test Bridge Types
Javier and his cousins talked about arch bridges, beam bridges, and suspension bridges. Try using pieces of paper, cardboard, and blocks to build an arch bridge and a beam bridge. Then try making a suspension bridge with two chairs and some string, just like they did in the story. Use heavy blocks, books, or toy cars to test your bridges. Which type of bridge is able to hold the most weight? Try making the span of each bridge thicker with sheets of cardboard. Does that make a difference?

Plan Your Bridge
Do you think you can improve one of the bridges that you tested so that it is even stronger? Remember what you learned when you tested the three different bridge types. Try to make your bridge strong in the areas where the bridges you tested were weak. Make a plan for the bridge that you would like to design.

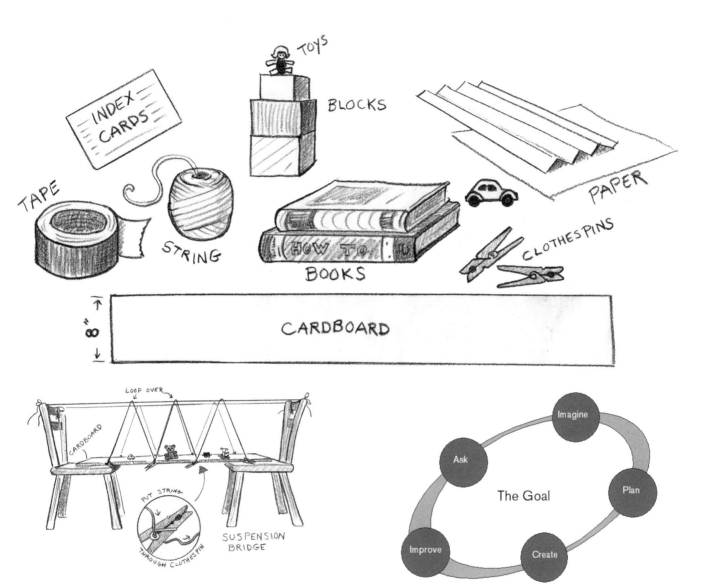

Create Your Bridge

Follow your plan and create the bridge that you designed. Once you have finished building, test your bridge. How many blocks can your bridge hold? Were you able to make your bridge strong in some of the places where the other bridges were weak?

Improve Your bridge

Use the engineering design process to improve your bridge. Go to the library and learn more about bridges. What are truss bridges? Platoon bridges? Try building with other materials like toothpicks, string, or popsicle sticks.

See What Others Have Done

See what other kids have done at http://www.mos.org/eie/tryit. What did you try? You can submit your solutions and pictures to our website, and maybe we'll post your submission!

Glossary

Abutment: The part of an arch bridge that stands at either end of the arch to maintain the arch's shape.

Arch bridge: A bridge made from one or more arches and abutments.

Beam bridge: A bridge made of a flat piece, or beam, laid across two or more supports or piers.

Civil engineering: The branch of engineering concerned with the design and construction of public structures, such as buildings, bridges, roads, and water systems.

Engineer: A person who uses his or her creativity and understanding of mathematics and science to design things that solve problems.

Engineering design process: The steps that engineers use to design something to solve a problem.

Masa: A type of dough made from corn that is often used in tortillas and tamales. Pronounced mah-seh.

Pier: A support for a beam bridge that helps hold up the beam.

Prototype: A model of a design that is made to help engineers understand and test the design.

Span: The length between two bridge supports.

Suspension bridge: A bridge made of a platform that is held up by wires or ropes strung from the tops of piers.

Tamale: A Mexican food made by steaming a mixture of meat, peppers, and spices in cornhusks. Pronounced teh-ma-lay.

Technology: Any thing or process that people create and use to solve a problem.